simply redwork

embroidery the hugs 'n kisses way

Landauer Publishing, LLC

 FACEBOOK.COM/
LANDAUERPUBLISHING
  YOUTUBE.COM/
LANDAUERPUBLISHING
 PINTEREST.COM/
LANDAUERPUB

simply redwork
embroidery the hugs' n kisses way
by Helen Stubbings, hugs'n kisses

Copyright © 2017 by Landauer Publishing, LLC

Projects Copyright © 2016
by Helen Stubbings, hugs'n kisses

This book was designed, produced,
and published by Landauer Publishing, LLC
3100 100th Street, Urbandale, IA 50322
515/287/2144   800/557/2144   landauerpub.com

President/Publisher: Jeramy Lanigan Landauer
Editor: Doris Brunnette
Art Director: Laurel Albright
Photographer: Sue Voegtlin

Library of Congress: 2017932159

ISBN 13:978-1-935726-91-3

Landauer Books are distributed to the Trade by
Fox Chapel Publishing
1970 Broad Street
East Petersburg, PA 17520
www.foxchapelpublishing.com
1-800-457-9112

For consumer orders:
Landauer Publishing, LLC
3100 100th Street
Urbandale, Iowa 50322
www.landauerpub.com
1-800-557-2144

This book printed on acid-free paper.

Printed in China

10-9-8-7-6-5-4-3-2-1

dedication

This book is dedicated to the many passionate and addicted stitchers across the world who, just like me, love the therapy of handwork. You stitch with me each night through the wonders of Facebook and Instagram, and share your passion through your lovely emails and face to face at classes, connecting us through this common love as I sit in my studio at the bottom of the world.

acknowledgements

To my sister, who continues to keep me sane, on target, on task and in a space of reason, thank you for your expertise, advice and voice of support.

To my beautiful family I hope I have managed to pass on some of my love of stitching. As you prepare to go out into the world, may you too have pins in your carpet and threads on your clothes.

My mum & dad who brought me up with a sense of purpose, to make a difference, to do what I dream and to find a way to make it happen.

To my hard working girls on the ground in our little Hugs 'n Kisses/Quarter Inch family, you keep the fires burning so that I may have the time to create, make and share.

contents

contents

introduction

From my early childhood years learning to stitch with my Grandmother, I have had a love of all crafts involving a needle and thread. I was honoured to inherit Grandma's fancywork box and from her, my appreciation of the therapy of stitching and the satisfaction of making something with my own hands. From a very young age I was mastering the lazy daisy, the stem stitch and cross stitch. Later, I hungrily expanded my stitchbook to include as many stitches and mediums as I could find.

In the 1880s, the introduction of a colorfast red thread from Turkey that was both cheaper than silk and easy to obtain, led to the trend of creating redwork items for the home. Turkey red thread was used typically on a muslin or light background cotton fabric. The lower class households used cotton fabric and inexpensive Turkey red thread to make embroidery and decorate their homes rather than using the silks and elaborate Crazy Quilt designs of the more landed gentry. Designs were simple line drawings including animals, children, kitchen and nature themes. They utilized basic stitches like the stem, outline, running and split stitches, French knots, backstitch, and lazy daisy stitch. The Kensington school for girls in England helped popularize redwork, hence the most common outline stitch is sometimes referred to as the Kensington Stitch. Redwork embroidery reached the peak of its popularity at the turn of the century and it remained in favor until the 1920s. In the early 1900s, redwork surged into America with Penny Squares — small squares of muslin stamped with a line drawing, that were sold for a penny a piece. In more recent years quilters have based whole quilts on this penny square style and have again brought about a revival in redwork.

one stitch at a time

Of course as more and more threads were manufactured with new technology, there were many more choices of quality, colorfast threads. Bluework became popular in the early 1900's, followed by other colors fashionable at the time. The technique can be completed using any color preference and in many thread types and weights.

When doing redwork, I prefer to use a variegated red thread as I feel it gives movement and depth to my designs. I have listed the thread types and colors used in each project. You may have others you prefer. However, to protect your project I do advise you to check the color fastness before use and/or follow the manufacturer's instructions when laundering. The many hand dyed threads available today are beautiful, but you may be disappointed if your project is ruined on the first wash.

I hope you enjoy the eclectic collection of projects and designs in this book. My aim was to include something for everyone, from traditional designs to projects with a modern aesthetic, whilst sharing my love of stitching. I want you to experience the therapeutic nature of handwork and satisfaction of making something with your very own hands.

my stitching philosphy is:

It feels good:

...to know we CAN make something with our own hands

...to see something we make finished and displayed or adored

...when others compliment our achievements

...when we give something we make to others and see their reaction

...to be able to show someone how we feel when to some this is difficult to express

...to be able to give strength or pleasure to others when we do this for them

...to bring that special feeling to individuals, families, communities and the world

I've found that stitching can build self esteem and self confidence, while fostering a caring and sharing attitude. Social media has made our world smaller, and provides a means to share our passions and our projects with friends around the globe! In that way, stitching can help reduce loneliness and isolation.

I am a believer that these projects are achievable by anyone, and stand by my motto that everything in life can be conquered just one stitch at a time.

xxx Helen

simply redwork

Embroidery:
the Hugs 'n Kisses way

Materials and tools :

Marking tools: I use a variety of marking tools. Some of my favorite include ceramic pencils (Sewline™ or similar), water soluble erasable pen or permanent fabric pen (Pigma Micron® pens work well), or a standard lead mechanical pencil.

Fabric: I have used good quality homespuns, muslins, linen, linen blends and 100% cotton tone on tone quilting fabrics throughout the book. I would encourage you to use the best quality fabric you can find for the best results.

Thread: The thread I used in each project is included in the requirements list. My favorites are all variegated reds, but if you prefer a solid red - DMC #498 is closest to the traditional Turkey red. The threads I used incude:

   Cottage Garden hand dyed thread
   #1007 Hugs 'n Kisses red - stranded floss
   Perle 12
   Cosmo Seasons thread #5006
   DMC 115 stranded floss
   Cosmo Perle #5 Cotton #346, 241, 242

Needles: I use a Hugs n' Kisses stitchery needle/ crewel needle for almost all of my redwork embroidery. It has a sharp point and a long eye, both important features. The sharp point allows your stitch to sit exactly where you want it, and the long eye makes threading the needle easier. The size of the needle depends on the size of the thread you are using. It needs to be large enough to make a hole so that your thread can pass through easily without dragging or wearing. If it is too large then it will leave holes in your fabric and your stitches will be loose and uneven. The larger the number, the smaller your needle. I use a #7 needle (Hugs 'n Kisses stitchery needle), which is the right size for 2-3 strands of floss or a size 12-16 Perle thread. For the size 5 Perle you will need a larger crewel needle.

Checkout my YouTube channel on tips for threading your needle using a never fail, first time every time method.

Embroidery hoop: I ALWAYS use an embroidery hoop, not so much for tension but as an extra hand to relieve stress from your wrist, elbow and shoulders. The hoop allows you to see where you are stitching and exactly where each needle insertion needs to be. The fabric does not need to be drum tight for redwork embroidery. It can be just a little slack, not stretched. I generally use a 6" to 8" hoop with my stitching method. You should be able to reach your fingers to the middle with your hand, holding the edge of the hoop. You may prefer not to use a hoop, but if you are new to stitching, I encourage you to start with a hoop.

Checkout my YouTube channel for hints on using your embroidery hoop and how to load it properly.

Stabilizer: I typically use a woven, lightweight stabilizer on the back of my embroidery work. It does several things: it keeps your tension neat and even and stops looser woven fabrics from moving/stretching as you pull a stitch through it. It allows you to begin and end with knots, and also to jump small distances between stitches. The choice of stabilizer will depend on your fabric and the end use of your embroidery.

Batting: Some of the projects in this book call for fusible batting as well as stabilizer. The battings I use include:

Vilene H630, Parlan, Stayflex, Shapeflex, Weaveline, Bosal #400 fashion fuse, Pellon® 987F Fusible Fleece, Bosal #426LF

Transferring designs:

There are many ways to transfer your design onto the fabric. The easiest method is to place your fabric onto a light box with the design underneath and use a marking tool to trace the design. My preference is a ceramic pencil (Sewline™ or similar) because it remains sharp and glides smoothly over the fabric. If your marking tool catches on the threads of the fabric, it can distort the design.

Another option is to use a transfer or graphite paper which comes in several colors. This works particularly well for darker fabrics. Another option for dark fabric is to use tulle netting. Use a sharpie to trace the design onto tulle, then place the tulle on your background fabric. Use a chalk pencil or ceramic marker to trace through the tulle over your sharpie design and onto the fabric. It will create dotted lines for you to stitch over. Trace your entire design before moving the fabric.

Stitching Methods:

There are two basic methods of stitching:

- The stab stitch: take the needle through the front of the fabric all the way through to the back, pull thread through until firm on the fabric, then bring the needle back up from the back to the front.

- The scoop stitch (my terminology): take the needle to the back and then up again to the front in one step. This is the method I use and I think it takes half the time; accomplishing two steps at once. This method uses the finger underneath to do most of the physical work.

Watch my Youtube Channel for a visual explanation of this method.

To knot or not to knot!?

If you are a Royal School of Needlework student or have the Embroidery police watching over you, then you have probably heard the phrase "the back should look as neat as the front". I am all about enjoying the process, getting something completed, feeling good about it and moving onto the next thing, not about being 'perfect' or what someone else deems to be correct. So, if it works for you, then by all means start and end your work with a knot. All of my projects are going to be made into something and have the back covered. No one will ever see the reverse side, and using stabilizer means your knots will not show.

Getting started

- Transfer your design to your chosen background fabric.
- Fuse stabilizer to the back of your fabric.
- Place your prepared piece into an embroidery hoop.
- Cut length of thread fingertip to elbow length (approximately 15"/38cm).
- Thread your needle (watch my YouTube video and you'll be an expert!)
- Knot the thread end.
- Stitch.

The process:

Follow the stitch guides in the book or choose your own stitches to cover all of your transferred lines.

Travelling: if you've used a stabilizer and are using a hoop feel free to jump from the end of one line or motif to the next without ending your thread and starting again. Now when I say jump, I mean maybe up to 1/4" or 6mm. Any more, you should weave the travelling thread through some other stitches so you don't leave a long, loose stitch to get snagged or caught later. If you are using a very sheer fabric this may not be possible as a dark red thread may shadow through and your jump will be visible from the front.

Ending: if your thread starts to wear, or is coming to its end, don't be stingy. Finish it off before it becomes tricky to do so. Wasting that extra inch will be worth it for an easy ending.

You have two choices to end:

- On the back, take the needle under the closest stitch and pull almost through, leaving a small loop. Pass the needle through the loop and tighten to form a knot. Repeat and clip thread close to the knot.

- On the back side, weave your thread along a row of stitches, taking it over and under each stitch at least 5-6 times to secure. Trim end close to fabric.

Finishing

Once you have finished and all marked lines have been stitched over, you are ready to make your embroidery into the chosen project, or perhaps into a project of your own.

Trim to size and press well. To press, use a soft towel and press with a steam iron, or press from the back on a soft surface. Trim any tails or threads on the back just in case they may shadow through the front and be visible.

the Hugs 'n Kisses way

Embroidery Stitch Guide

For more assistance with embroidery stitches please visit www.hugsnkisses.typepad.com/hugsfromhelen/stitchedsunday/

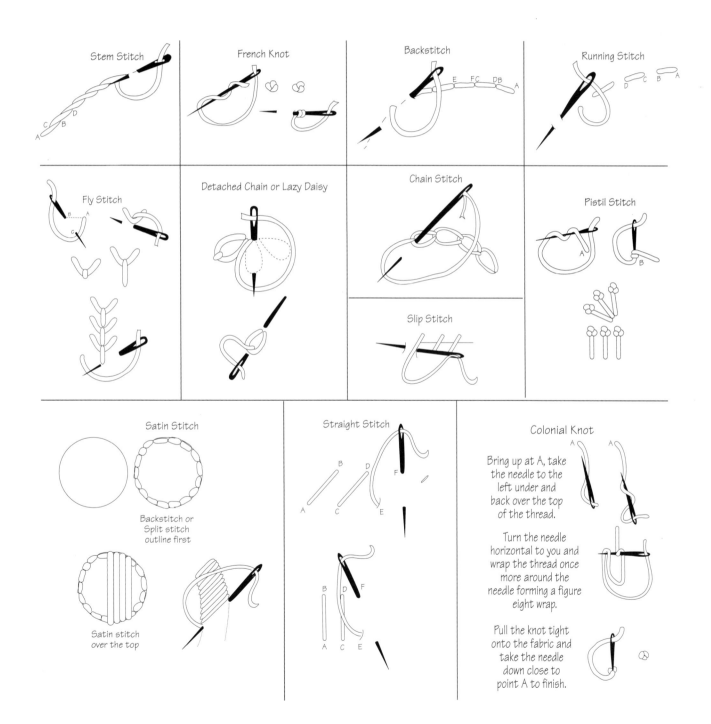

penny square quilt

Quilt measures approximately 25"/64cm square

requirements

5/8 yd/50cm white background fabric

4 fat quarters various red tone on tone prints

4 fat quarters white/red prints

1/4 yd/22cm binding fabric

fusible stabilizer

30" square/75cm batting

7/8 yd/82cm backing

Cosmo Seasons #5006 floss, or any six strand variegated red embroidery floss

cutting

From each fat quarter cut:

Three—1-1/2" x 22" strips

(from one of the red fat quarters, cut an extra 1-1/2" x 22" strip)

From white background fabric cut:

16—6" x 6" squares

From binding fabric cut:

Three—2-1/2" x wof strips

notes...

I used various coordinating fabrics from my stash to make this traditional style penny square quilt.

Historically the white fabrics were purchased as printed muslin squares and cost one penny, hence the name. I have bordered them with a 1" checkerboard sashing using a variety of red and white tone on tone fabrics. You just need to choose some that 'read' red and some that 'read' white.

I used Cosmo Seasons stranded floss in color #5006 - two strands were used to stitch over all lines.

step by step

1 Transfer design onto fabric using your preferred method (page 9).

2 Fuse stabilizer to the wrong side.

3 Place a fabric square into your embroidery hoop and stitch over all transferred lines following the design. Refer to embroidery stitch guide on page 11.

4 Once finished press each square and trim to 5-1/2", centering the design.

stitches used...

Lazy Daisy/Colonial Knot

Straight Stitch

Backstitch

penny square quilt

5 Join red and white/red strips together into strip sets (Diagram 1). Press seams toward the red fabric. Make two Strip Set A and three Strip Set B.

Diagram 1

Make 2
Strip Set A

Make 3
Strip Set B

6 From Strip Set A, cut a total of (15) 1-1/2" x 5-1/2" A units. From Strip Set B, cut a total of (30) 1-1/2" x 5-1/2" B units (Diagram 2).

Diagram 2

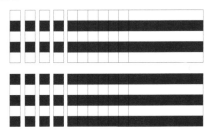

7 Join three A units and two B units, alternating between sets to make a row of sashing. Make five rows (Diagram 3).

Diagram 3

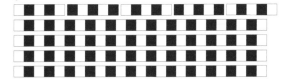

8 Join the 20 remaining B units to sides of stitched panels, Make four rows. Press seams toward the pieced strips (Diagram 4).

Diagram 4

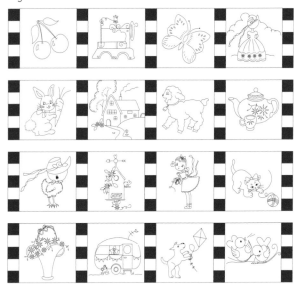

9 Join rows with sashing rows from step 7, pressing seams toward sashing. Attach final sashing rows to top and bottom. Press toward sashing (Diagram 5).

Diagram 5

10 Layer for quilting according to instructions on page 75.

11 Quilt as desired. I kept the quilting quite simple by using white thread and quilting in the ditch of all sashing and border strips. The white thread blends into the fabric.

daisy chain pouch

requirements

5" x 11"/13 x 30cm natural linen

10-1/2" x 20"/25 x 50cm striped toweling

10-1/2" x 22"/25 x 55cm lining fabric

3" x 5"/8 x 13cm linen for tab

12"/30cm zipper

5" x 11"/13 x 30cm woven stabilizer
Fusible batting (lightweight) 10-1/2" x 22"/25 x 55cm

Cottage Garden Perle 12 #1007 Hugs n' Kisses red, or any variegated red Perle cotton

cutting

From striped toweling cut:

(2) 3" x 10-1/2" strips

(1) 9-1/2" x 10-1/2" rectangle

From lining fabric cut:

(2) 9-1/2" x 10-1/2" rectangles

From batting, cut:

(2) 9-1/2" x 10-1/2" rectangles

step by step

1 Transfer design onto fabric using your preferred method (page 9). Fuse lightweight woven stablizer to wrong side. Place into embroidery hoop and stitch over all transferred lines following the embroidery stitch guide (page 11). Once complete, press well and trim to 4-1/2" x 10-1/2", centering your stitched design.

2 Attach a 3" x 10-1/2" rectangle of striped fabric to the top and bottom of the stitched panel. Press seams toward stripe. This panel should now measure 9-1/2" x 10-1/2".

3 Baste or fuse the ligthweight batting to the wrong side of the 9-1/2" x 10-1/2"stitched panel. You may choose to quilt through both of these panels. I quilted straight lines in the red stripes of the towelling fabric with red thread.

4 Fold the 3" x 5" rectangle in half lengthwise and press. Open and fold each raw edge in to meet the center fold. Fold in half so raw edges are tucked inside. Edgestitch using a matching thread down each side. Fold in half, aligning raw edges and pin to front panel approximately 1" from top edge. Baste in place.

5 Place outer bag panel right side up on work surface. Position zipper, teeth down, along the top aligning raw edges. Place lining fabric on top of zipper, right side down and, pin (Diagram 1). Note: I have suggested a longer than necessary zipper so you will have more overhanging at each end. This allows you to join outer bag, zipper and lining without having to stitch past and around a zipper pull.

Diagram 1

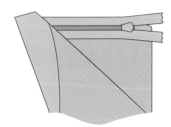

6 Stitch using a zipper foot as close to the teeth as possible. Open out outer panel and lining on both sides of zipper (Diagram 2). Press each panel well. Repeat this process with the remaining outer panel and lining along other side of the zipper.

Diagram 2

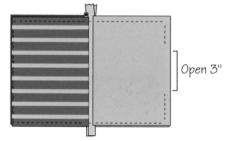

7 Open the zipper about half way along top of the bag. Place bag on work surface so that the two outer bag panels are right sides together and all outer edges are even; pin. Do the same with the two lining pieces. You will fold the top seam allowances and zipper tape toward the lining. Pin, matching all seams. Stitch around the outer edge of the bag leaving a 3" opening in one side of the lining only (Diagram 3).

Diagram 3

Open 3"

8 Fold each corner flat, matching seams, to form a triangle; pin. Stitch across each corner 1-1/2" from the point. Trim excess (Diagram 4).

Diagram 4

9 Turn bag right side out by pulling through the opening in the side of the lining, then slip stitch closed. Press all seams and corners well. Push lining to the inside of the outer bag through the zipper.

Bag measures approximately 7-1/2 x 10"/18 x 26 cm

stitches used...

Satin Stitch

Colonial Knot

Backstitch

welcome

Framed print measures 12"/30cm square

requirements

12"/30cm square muslin for background

Picture frame with opening of
approximately 9"/22cm square

12"/30cm square woven stabilizer

Cottage Garden floss #1007 Hugs 'n Kisses
red, or any six strand red variegated floss

step by step

1 Transfer design onto fabric using your preferred method (page 9). Fuse stabilizer to the wrong side following the manufacturer's instructions.

2 Place panel into embroidery hoop. Stitch over all drawn lines following the embroidery stitch guide (page 11), using two strands of floss.

3 Once finished, press well.

4 Remove the back of the picture frame and choose the thickest board inside. If this is not sturdy enough, use it as a template to cut a piece of heavier backing.

5 Postion the board centrally over the back of the embroidery panel. Referring to diagram on page 33, lace the fabric over the card using a long thread and a large needle. Lace horizontally first, pulling firmly so fabric is taut, turn to front and adjust so the design is perfectly centered. Continue to lace vertically.

6 Place the embroidery into the frame and secure.

hint I chose to dye my muslin to give it an aged look. I used Parisian Browning Essence in hot water, and let the fabric air dry. You could achieve the same look by tea-dying.

notes...

This cute little welcome house has been framed to suit a country style home. You could add borders and make a little wallhanging or turn it into a pillow cover. It could even be used as a panel in a quilt or a bag. Of course, changing the fabric could give it a new look. For this project, I used two strands of Cottage Garden hand dyed floss in #1007 Hugs 'n Kisses red.

stitches used...

Backstitch

Satin Stitch

love, live, laugh

Each banner measures approximately
4-3/4" x 8"/12 x 20cm

requirements

10" x 18"/25 x 45cm background fabric

2" x 16"/5 x 40cm red gingham

10" x 18"/25 x 45cm backing fabric

10" x 18"/25 x 45cm Stabilizer - (lightweight fusible batting)

Cosmo Seasons floss #5006, or any six strand variegated red embroidery floss

cutting

From backing fabric cut:
  (3) 5-1/4" x 7-3/4" rectangles

From red gingham cut:
  (3) 2" x 5-1/4" rectangles

step by step

1 Transfer design onto fabric using your preferred method (page 9), leaving about 1" between designs. Fuse stabilizer to the wrong side following manufacturer's instructions.

2 Stitch over all drawn lines following the embroidery stitch guide (page 11).

3 When finished stitching, cut apart and trim each design to measure 5-1/4" x 7-3/4", ensuring each design is centered.

4 Double fold 1/4" toward wrong side of fabric on each end of a 2" x 5-1/4" red gingham strip. Edgestitch using a matching thread. Press in half wrong sides together.

5 Align raw edges and center the tab at the top edge of the stitched panel; pin.

6 Place stitched panel right sides together with backing fabric. Stitch around outside edges leaving a generous opening in the bottom edge. Clip the corners and turn right side out through the opening; open out all seams and corners well.

7 Slip stitch the opening closed and press the piece.

8 Repeat steps 4-7 for the other two banners. Place the banners onto the stand by inserting the split rod into the tab opening.

notes...

These banners were designed to fit the Ackfeld Wire 4" x 9" tri-stand. You could, of course, use these little designs in many other ways. Add borders, use them in a bag project or frame them. The choice is yours!

notes...

I have used tone on tone quilting cotton to stitch my designs and a single Strand of Cosmo Seasons #5006 floss, as the designs are very small in scale.

For the tab I used red gingham from my stash. I used a Parlan stabilizer so that when stitched and turned I already had some loft in my banner. This is a very lightweight fusible batting product.

love, live, laugh

stitches used...

French/Colonial Knot for eyes

Backstitch

live like there is no tomorrow—love like you have
dream like there are no impossibilities—sing as if

Laugh like no-one is listening
listening
dream like there are no impossibilities

Sing as if no-one can hear
dance as if no-one is watching

*never been hurt—laugh like no-one is listening—
no-one can hear—dance as if no-one is watching*

simply sweet purse

Purse measures 7" x 8"/18 x 20 cm

requirements

1/3 yard/30.5cm linen background

1/4 yard/23cm lining fabric

12"/30cm square stabilizer

6"/15cm spring clip flex purse frame

Purse chain (optional)

Cottage Garden Perle size 12 #1007 Hugs 'n Kisses red, or any six strand variegated red embroidery floss

cutting

From linen fabric cut:

(1) 12" x 12" square embroidery background

(4) 2-1/2" x 6-1/2" strips for purse top

(1) Purse Back from Simply Sweet Purse Template (page 26)

From lining fabric cut:

(2) from Simply Sweet Purse Template

step by step

1 Transfer design, including outer template line, onto 12" linen square using your preferred method (page 9). Fuse lightweight woven stabilizer to the wrong side, following manufacturer's instructions.

2 Place into embroidery hoop and stitch over all lines following the embroidery stitch guide (page 11). Do not stitch template cutting line.

3 Press well and trim to template cutting line. Place the purse front and back right sides together. Sew along curved edge, clip curves and turn right side out.

4 Place two lining pieces right sides together, sew a 1/4" seam along sides of lining, leaving a generous opening along bottom edge for turning. Clip curves.

5 To make the top casings, stitch (2) 2-1/2" x 6-1/2" strips right sides together along short ends. Turn through and press. Fold in half lengthwise. Repeat for other casing.

6 On each side of the purse opening, pin casing strips, aligning raw edges, to top of the purse.

7 With right sides together, place embroidered bag with pinned casings inside the lining, matching top and side seams. Stitch around top of bag opening. Turn bag through opening in lining, press and slip stitch closed.

8 Insert spring strip through casings, insert pin to join strips, and close bag top. Bend over the tiny flap on the spring strip end to enclose pin.

notes...

I have used a spring clip flex frame with purse loops so that I could attach a long purse chain. You may prefer to make your own version of a strap or handle, or simply use it as a pouch.

simply sweet purse

Simply Sweet Purse Template

stitches used...

All other Backstitch

Stem Stitch

Satin Stitch

Colonial Knot

Chain Stitch

Chain Stitch

Stem Stitch

Colonial Knot

Running Stitch

Satin Stitch

high tea

Tea cloth measures 34"/86cm square

Napkins measure 11"/28cm square

requirements - for cloth and 2 napkins

1-5/8 yard/1.45m red gingham (min 42" wide)

1-3/8 yard/115cm white fabric

lightweight woven stabilizer

Presencia Finca Perle size 16 #1490, or other red size 16 Perle Cotton

cutting instructions

From white fabric cut:
    (1) 35" x 35" square for tea cloth
    (2) 12" x 12" squares for napkins

From red gingham cut:
    (1) 42" x 42" square for tea cloth back
    (2) 15" x 15" squares for napkin backs

step by step

1 Transfer design onto fabric using your preferred method (page 9). Fold the 35" square fabric into quarters and finger press the folds to find the center. Transfer center circle design onto the central position.

2 Measure 3" in from each corner and mark to position the corner motifs (Diagram 1). Place a large basket in opposite corners and a small flower spray in the remaining two corners.

3 Fuse lightweight stabilizer on the back of each design, following manufacturer's instructions.

4 Place a design into the embroidery hoop and stitch over all transferred lines using a single strand of the Perle #16 thread. Repeat steps 3-4 for napkins.

stitches used...

Lazy Daisy/Colonial Knot

Running Stitch

Backstitch

Diagram 1

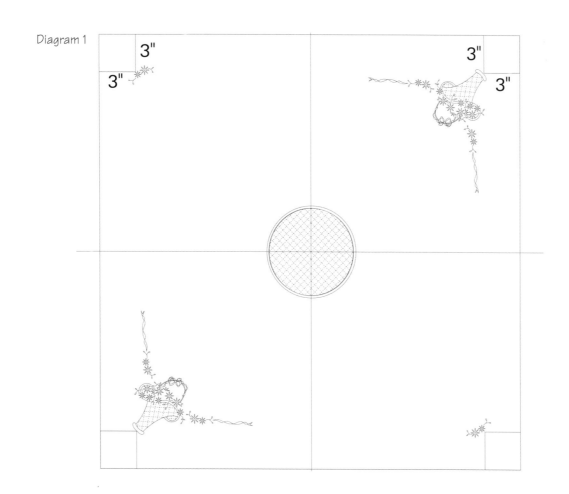

5 Once complete, press well. Trim the tea cloth to 34" square and the napkins to 11" square.

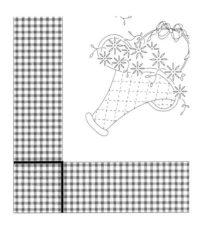

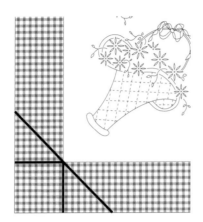

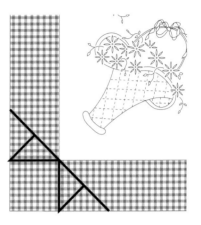

6 With wrong sides together, smooth and center embroidered tea cloth on top of red gingham fabric. There should be 4" of gingham showing on all sides. With a water-soluble pen or ceramic pencil, draw a vertical and horizontal line from the corner of the white fabric, as shown. Note: Instructions are same for the napkins, except there should be 2" of red gingham showing on all sides.

7 Using the 45° line of a cutting ruler, draw a line at a 45° angle across corner, as shown.

8 Using your ruler, draw a line 90° from the edge of the gingham to the center of the 45° line on each side, as shown.

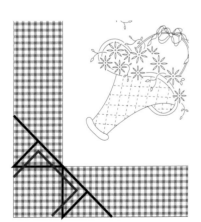

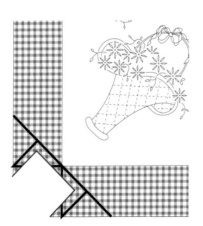

9 Using your ruler, draw a line 1/4" inside drawn lines as shown.

10 Cut along drawn 1/4" line and remove corner fabric. Set stitchery aside.

11 Repeat on all corners of tea cloth and napkins.

12 Fold right sides of gingham over as shown (Diagram 2). Stitch with 1/4" seam on two sides of cutout. Repeat with all corners.

Diagram 2

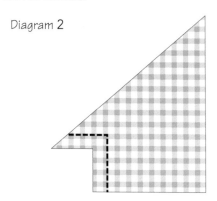

notes...

For serving high tea, or impressing grandmother, a vintage style tea cloth and napkins is sure to do the trick. Backed with a classic red gingham, I have used a double-folded mitered technique so it is backed to hide the stitches. I used Presencia Finca Perle #16 red thread (single strand) #1490 to stitch this traditional fancywork design.

13 Turn corners right side out. Fold raw edge back to fold created by corner. (Diagram 3). Press to form crisp, creased edges. Repeat steps 12-13 for napkins.

Diagram 3

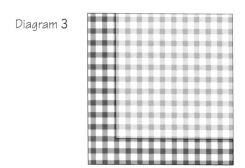

14 Insert the well pressed embroidery fabric inside gingham backing, centering and tucking nicely under the folded edges. The embroidery fabric should meet the inside edges snugly but sit flat. If not, trim it back a little as the folded gingham edge will cover it.

15 Pin outer edges through all layers. Edgestitch with blending thread. Press tea cloth and napkins well.

yuletide

A few notes on inspiration:

Inspiration surrounds us; I see designs in everything in life. I am influenced by the skills, history and design elements of other cultures such as Hungarian or Scandinavian traditional embroidery. Elements of architecture and furniture design are also very rich with inspiration, even stone carvings in old cemeteries. Other avenues are three-dimensional and home decor products. Yuletide is an example of this, inspired by a 3D gold Christmas tree table ornament. Look around you, open your eyes to the possibilities and you too will be inspired to make your own stitched designs. Always carry a camera or smart phone and start collecting ideas or things that inspire you!

Frame measures 10" x 12"/25 x 30cm

requirements

15" x 17"/38cm x 43cm natural linen

Purchased frame approx 10" x 12"/25x30cm

2 skeins Cottage Garden Perle size 12 #1007 Hugs 'n Kisses red, or other red size 12 Perle cotton

step by step

1 Transfer design onto fabric using your preferred method (page 9).

2 Fuse lightweight woven interfacing to the wrong side of linen, following manufacturer's instructions. Place into embroidery hoop.

3 Stitch over all drawn lines following the embroidery stitch guide (page 11).

4 Remove the back of the picture frame and choose the thickest board inside. If this is not sturdy enough, use it as a template to cut a piece of heavier backing.

5 Postion the board centrally over the back of the embroidery panel. Lace the fabric over the card using a long thread and a large needle. Lace horizontally first, pulling firmly so fabric is taut, turn to front and adjust so the design is perfectly centered. Continue to lace vertically.

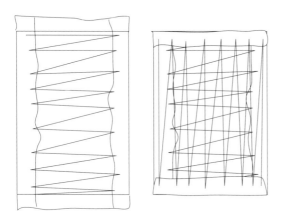

6 Place the embroidery into the frame and secure.

stitches used...

Backstitch

Satin Stitch

loving minis

Frames measure approximately 2" x 3"/5 x 7cm

requirements

6" x 18"/15 x 45cm white tone on tone fabric

Cottage Garden Perle size 12 #1007 Hugs 'n Kisses red, or other red size 12 Perle cotton

Set of three mini frames

cutting

I did not precut my background fabric. Instead, I completed my stitching as one large piece, trimming it to size after completion.

notes...

On finding these cute little frames in a dollar store, I had to have them! This was a set of three, so I drew simple little designs to fit them. If you find frames that are slightly different in size, adjust the designs to fit. Or, you might want to do your own little drawings. Alternatively, border the designs to make mini wallhangings, pincushions or lavender pillows. Use your imagination and live, love & laugh.

step by step

1 Transfer design onto fabric using your preferred method (page 9). Allow approximately 3"-4" between designs.

2 Fuse lightweight woven stabilizer to the wrong side following manufacturer's instructions.

3 Stitch over all drawn lines following the embroidery stitch guide (page 11).

4 Once complete press well and trim each design to fit your frames, centering each design.

5 Remove the back of the picture frame. If there is not a sturdy backing piece included, make a template from the glass or paper to cut a strong backing.

Referring to the diagram on page 33, lace the stitched design over the backing, ensuring you have the design centered. Place it into the frame and check through the window to see that it is centered. Tie off the lacing, insert into frame and secure.

stitches used...

Backstitch

Cross Stitch

Colonial Knot   Running Stitch

perfect pair

Each cushion measures 14"/36cm square

requirements (for two cushions)

3/8 yard/38cm tan linen

3/8 yard/38cm red decorator fabric

1/2 yard/45cm backing fabric

lightweight woven stabilizer

Cottage Garden Perle size 12 #1007
Hugs 'n Kisses red, or other red size 12
Perle cotton

cutting

From tan linen cut:

(2) 5" x 15" rectangles for cushion edges

(1) 10-1/2" x 14-1/2" rectangle for tan cushion

From red decorator fabric cut:

(1) 10-1/2" x 14-1/2" rectangle for red cushion

(1) 1" x 14-1/2" strip for trim on tan cushion

Choose your preferred method of making a cushion back from options on page 79-80. Cut backing fabrics to suit.

step by step

1 Transfer the designs to the 5" x 15" fabric using your preferred method (page 9).

2 Fuse lightweight woven stabilizer to the back, following manufacturer's instructions. Place into embroidery hoop.

3 Stitch over all drawn lines following the embroidery stitch guide (page 11).

4 Press well and trim each panel to measure 4-1/2" x 14-1/2".

5 **Tan cushion:** Fold and press 1" x 14-1/2" decorator fabric in half, wrong sides together. Place right sides together with fold toward vine embroidery strip; pin. Position the 10-1/2" x 14-1/2"linen piece, right sides together aligning raw edges. Stitch using a 1/4" seam allowance. Press open with red flange pointing away from embroidery.

6 **Red cushion:** Attach the 10-1/2" x 14-1/2" piece of decorator fabric to remaining embroidery panel, aligning raw edges; stitch. Press seam toward linen.

7 Complete the cushions using your preferred method on page 79-80. Insert pillow forms or stuff.

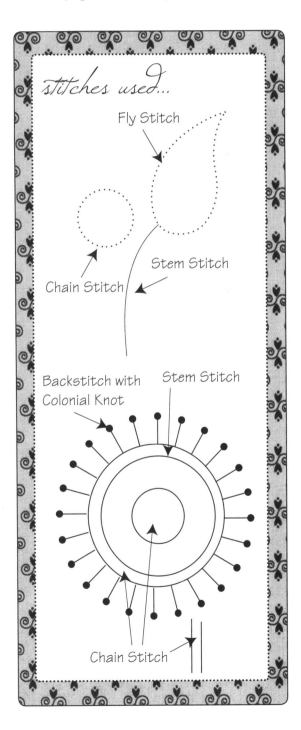

stitches used...

Fly Stitch

Chain Stitch

Stem Stitch

Backstitch with Colonial Knot

Stem Stitch

Chain Stitch

mollymook ipad pouch

Finished size approximately 9" x 11"/ 23 x 28cm

requirements

1/3 yard/30cm striped linen

6" x 8"/15 x 20cm natural linen

1/3 yard/30cm lining

3" x 7"/8 x 18cm red floral

Lightweight fusible batting

Lightweight woven stabilizer

1yd/1m red ric rac

Cottage Garden Perle size 12 #1007
Hugs 'n Kisses red, or other red size
12 Perle cotton

1/2"/18mm magnet clasp

cutting

From striped linen cut:
(1) 9-1/2" x 22-1/2" rectangle for pouch

From lining fabric cut:
(1) 9-1/2" x 22-1/2" rectangle

From red tab fabric cut:
one piece 3" x 7"

From lightweight fusible batting cut:
(1) 9-1/2" x 22-1/2" rectangle

This simple but lovely iPad or Kindle pouch can be adjusted to fit any device. Check the measurements of your tablet before cutting and adjust the measurements to suit. I have used a strong bag magnet to close my tab. However, if you are more adventurous you may choose to insert a zipper or other type of closure. You could, of course, also make this without the embroidery.

step by step

1 Transfer the design to the 6" x 8" fabric using your preferred method (page 9).

2 Fuse lightweight woven stabilizer to the back following manufacturer's instructions. Place into embroidery hoop.

3 Stitch over all drawn lines following the embroidery stitch guide (page 11). Do not stitch outer cutting line. Press well and cut out on outer border line.

4 On the right side of embroidery, position ric rac so it covers outer edge. Stitch with 1/4" seam through the center of ric rac, making sure there are no gaps showing (Diagram 1). Overlap cut ends.

5 Turn the ric rac to the back of embroidery design, along the stitch line. This will give a neat, turned oval edge. Press well.

stitches used...

Running Stitch

Backstitch

Diagram 1

mollymook ipad pouch

6 Position the oval panel as shown in Diagram 2. Glue or pin baste. Using a matching red thread, stitch into place in the ditch between the ric rac and the linen edge of embroidery panel.

Diagram 2

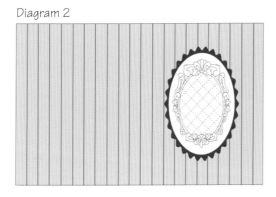

7 Fuse lightweight fusible batting to the wrong side of the striped linen.

8 With right sides together, fold the 3" x 7" floral rectangle in half to make a 3" x 3-1/2" tab. Stitch two long sides. Clip corners, turn to right side and press well. Edgestitch around three closed sides.

9 Insert one side of magnet into tab, centering towards the end of the tab (Diagram 3). Follow manufacturer's instructions to anchor magnet.

Diagram 3

10 Position tab at the top edge of the pouch, magnet facing up, and centered with the embroidered oval (Diagram 4). Baste in place.

Diagram 4

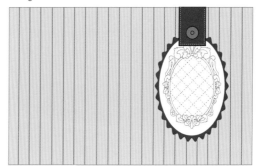

11 Fold panel in half and match magnet position on the back side of linen (Diagram 5). Insert other half of magnet, following manufacturer's instructions to anchor.

Diagram 5

12 With right sides together, sew lining to the top long edge of the linen panel. The tab will be sandwiched in between. Open and press well with seam pressed toward the linen (Diagram 6).

Diagram 6

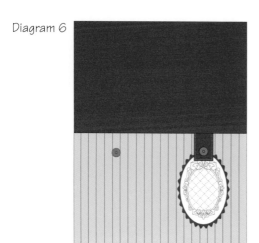

13 With right sides together, fold pouch into a tube (Diagram 7) and stitch around all edges, leaving a generous opening in the lining side of pouch.

Diagram 7

Leave open

14 Clip the corners and turn right side out through the opening in the lining. Press seams and corners well and slip stitch the opening closed.

15 Push lining smoothly down inside the outer pouch. You may like to edgestitch around the top of your pouch to ensure the lining lays flat. Insert your iPad or Kindle and close the tab.

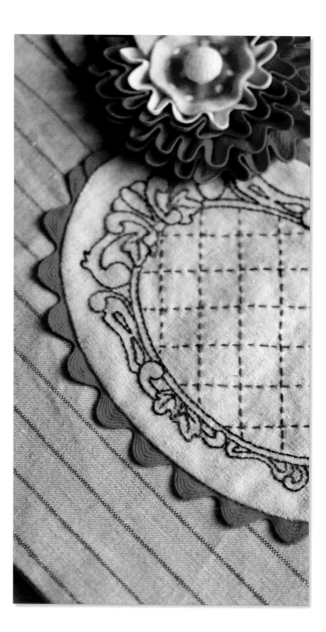

ramblin' rose cushion

Cushion measures 15"/38cm square

requirements

1/2 yard/45cm linen

1/2 yard/45cm backing

lightweight woven stabilizer

Cottage Garden Perle size 12 #1007
Hugs 'n Kisses red (note:I used several skeins),
or other red size 12 Perle cotton.

cutting

From linen fabric cut:
  One 16" x 16" square

Choose your preferred method of making a
cushion back from options on page 79-80.
Cut backing fabrics to suit.

step by step

1 Transfer design onto fabric using your preferred method (page 9).

2 Fuse lightweight woven stabilizer to the wrong side, following the manufacturer's instructions.

3 Stitch over all drawn lines following the embroidery stitch guide (page 11).

4 Press well, and trim to measure 15-1/2" x 15-1/2", centering design.

5 Complete your cushion using your preferred method on page 79-80. Insert pillow form or stuff.

hint The Fly Stitch used in this design can take a little practice to get the nice, curved leaf shape. It is important to keep the V angle of the stitches in the leaf. Don't let them become too 'straight'.

The design also creates a long stitch which can be snagged and pulled so take care when laundering.

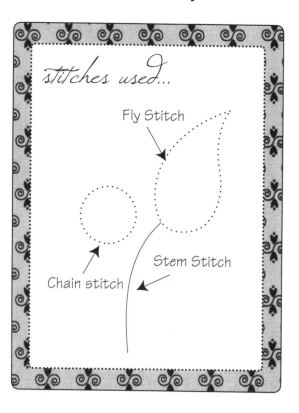

stitches used...

Fly Stitch

Chain stitch

Stem Stitch

my house

Cushion measures 15"/38cm square

requirements

1/2 yard/45cm linen

1/2 yard/45cm backing

Cottage Garden floss #1007 Hugs 'n Kisses red, or other variegated red floss.

Lightweight fusible woven stabilizer

Acetate clear plastic sheet

cutting

From linen cut:
   One 16" x 16" square

Choose your preferred method of making a cushion back from options on page 79-80. Cut backing fabrics to suit.

step by step

1 Take a photograph of your home or subject.

2 Print it on a photocopier or printer in black and white, enlarged to the desired design size.

3 Place a sheet of clear acetate over the photograph and using a Sharpie marker, trace over the main lines. Trace only what you want to stitch to give a simplified yet recognizable design to stitch.

4 Transfer design onto fabric using your preferred method (page 9).

5 Fuse lightweight woven stabilizer to the back of your linen following manufacturer's instructions. Place into embroidery hoop.

6 Stitch over all drawn lines following the embroidery stitch guide (page 11). My House was completed with a simple backstitch on the design.

7 Once complete, press well and follow your preferred method from pages 79-80 to finish your cushion cover. Insert pillow form or stuff.

notes...

This lovely cushion was made for me by my daugther Molly, for my birthday. She designed the stitchery using a method that is simple and achievable by all. Make your own design of your home, your child, your garden, anything you desire. Make it personal and create a family heirloom! Molly used two strands of Cottage Garden floss and a simple backstitch to complete the embroidery. What a special gift this was, having no idea she had photographed, designed and stitched this just for me, and knowing that I have managed to pass on my love of design, stitching and giving to my daughter!

I have given the general instructions on how to do this for yourself, (not the pattern for my cushion) you will need to use your own subject to design your own version.

stitches used...

Backstitch

under the mulberry tree

Hoop measures 10"/26cm

requirements
14"/30cm square natural linen

DMC #115 variegated floss, or other
variegated red floss

lightweight woven stabilizer

Clear craft glue

10"/26cm embroidery hoop

step by step

1 Transfer design onto fabric using your preferred method (page 9).

2 Fuse lightweight stabilizer to the back of the linen following manufacturer's instructions.

3 Using two strands, place into embroidery hoop and stitch on all traced lines following the embroidery stitch guide (page 11). Press well.

4 After pressing, place into large display embroidery hoop and center the design; pull until taut but do not stretch. Turn over and trim fabric to approximately 1" from the edge of the hoop.

5 Place glue on inside edge of inner hoop. Fold fabric in and press onto the glue; let dry.

stitches used...

Running Stitch

Backstitch

mini coin purse

Coin purse measures 4"/10cm high

requirements

8"/20cm square natural linen

8"/20cm square lining

lightweight woven stabilizer

Cottage Garden floss #1007 Hugs 'n Kisses red, or other variegated red floss

One 2"/5cm sew-in purse frame

step by step

1 Transfer design onto fabric using your preferred method (page 9). Trace the outer cutting line and mark the small dashes (Diagram 1).

Diagram 1

2 Fuse lightweight stabilizer to the wrong side of panel following manufacturer's instructions.

3 Stitch over all drawn lines following the embroidery stitch guide (page 11), using a single strand of floss.

4 Press linen well and trim to the outer template line. On lining fabric, trace along outer cutting line to make two lining pieces. Trim and mark the small dashes.

5 With right sides together, align front and back of purse. Stitch, ending at the line markings, as shown (Diagram 2).

Diagram 2

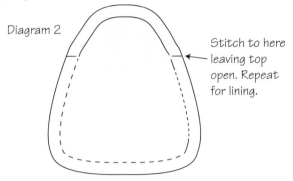

Stitch to here leaving top open. Repeat for lining.

6 Repeat with lining pieces leaving a small opening in bottom edge for turning (Diagram 3)

Diagram 3

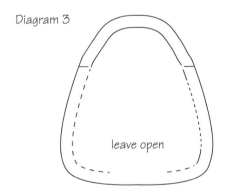

leave open

7 With right sides together, place outer bag inside lining. Sew along top edges.

8 Turn through opening in lining, press and slip stitch closed.

9 Insert top edges into purse frame and stitch through the holes in the purse frame using a strong thread and a back stitch.

hint There are many purse frames available for purchase. If your frame is a different size or shape, adjust the template slightly to suit. You can also get glue-in frames that don't have the holes to stitch through. Follow the manufacturer's instructions for assembly.

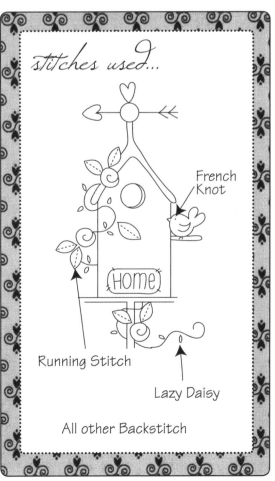

stitches used...

French Knot

Running Stitch

Lazy Daisy

All other Backstitch

happy times tote

Bag measures 15"w x 6"d x 15"h/38 x 15 x 38 cm

requirements

9"/23cm square white fabric

3/8 yard/33cm red dot fabric

1/2 yard/45cm red/white floral fabric

3/8 yard/33cm red/white text fabric

3/4 yard/68cm lining fabric

3/4 yard/68cm single sided fusible batting

1 yd/1m red ric rac

Cottage Garden Perle size 12 #1007 Hugs 'n Kisses red, or other red size 12 Perle cotton

cutting

From red dot fabric cut:
   (1) 10-1/2"X 15-1/2" rectangle
   for outer bag

   (2) 4-1/2" x 21" strips for handles

From red/white floral cut:
   (2) 3" x 15-1/2" strips for outer bag
   (1) 15-1/2" square for outer bag

From red/white text fabric cut:
   (3) 6-1/2" x 15-1/2" rectangles
   for outer bag

From lining cut:
   (2) 15-1/2" squares
   (3) 6-1/2" x 15-1/2" rectangles

From batting cut:
   (2) 15-1/2"squares
   (3) 6-1/2" x 15-1/2" rectangles
   (2) 1" x 21" strips for handles

step by step

1 Transfer the design to the center of the fabric using your preferred method (page 9). Fuse woven stabilizer to the wrong side, following manufacturer's instructions. Place into embroidery hoop.

2 Stitch over all drawn lines following the embroidery stitch guide (page 11). Do not stitch outer cutting line. Press well and cut on outer line.

3 On the right side of embroidery, position ric rac so it covers outer edge. Stitch with 1/4" seam through the center of ric rac, making sure there are no gaps showing (Diagram 1). Overlap cut ends of ric rac.

4 Turn the ric rac to the back of embroidery design, along the stitch line. This will give a neat, turned circle edge. Press well.

notes...

This tote is a great size to take shopping or to carry your supplies for a sit and sew gathering. I have used fun stitch themed coordinating quilting fabrics for my bag. The bag batting, which holds its shape well, can easily be stitched or quilted through. Mine was a fusible batting but you could use a non-fusible version and add more quilting to each panel during the construction of your bag. It will come together very quickly and you'll want to make more than one!

Diagram 1

5 Position circle panel in the center of the 10-1/2" x 15-1/2" red dot rectangle. Glue or pin baste. Stitch in the ditch of the white background and ric rac, using a matching red thread.

stitches used...

Lazy Daisy   Colonial Knot

Backstitch

Satin Stitch

happy times tote

7 Attach a 3" x 15" red/white floral strip to both sides of the red dot fabric. Press toward dot fabric (Diagram 2).

Diagram 2

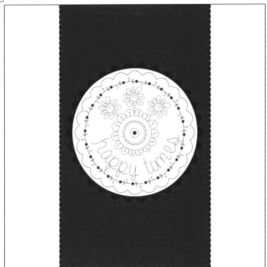

Front Bag Panel

8 Following the manufacturer's instructions, fuse bag batting to the wrong side of the front bag panel, the three 6-1/2" x 15-1/2" red/white text rectangles, and the 15-1/2" red/white floral square for the back panel.

9 If desired, quilt your front and back panels. I used a walking foot, and quilted in-the-ditch on both sides of the front center panel and quilted vertical lines, 1" apart, on back bag panel (Diagram 3).

Diagram 3

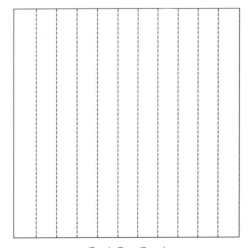

Back Bag Panel

10 Join three 6-1/2" x 15" floral rectangles together, making one long strip for side panels and bottom of bag.

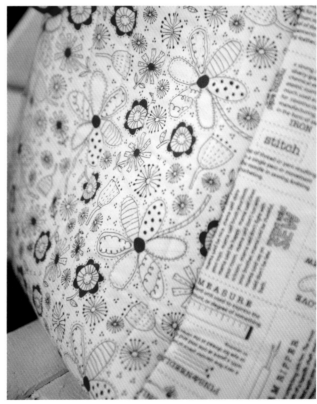

11 Beginning at a top edge, attach long strip to the front panel stopping 1/4" from the bottom edge (Diagram 4).

Diagram 4

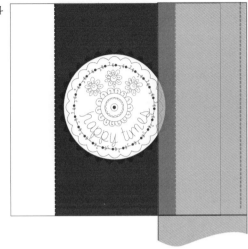

12 With needle down, lift the presser foot and pivot. Stitch along bottom edge, pivot (Diagram 5).

Diagram 5

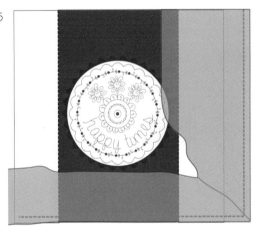

13 Stitch other side finishing at the top edge (Diagram 6). Repeat, sewing side panels to back panel.

Diagram 6

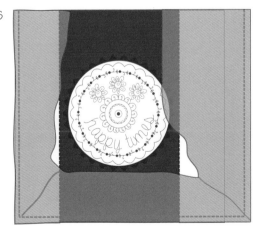

happy times tote

14 Repeat steps 10-13 using lining pieces. Make a long side panel strip and join to both 15-1/2" lining squares. Leave a generous opening in one of the side seams (Diagram 7).

Diagram 7

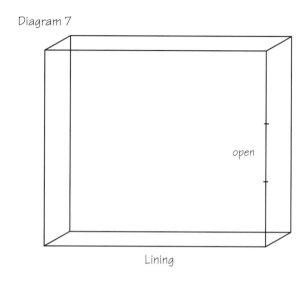

open

Lining

15 To make handles (Diagram 8), fold the 4-1/2" x 21" red dot strip in half lengthwise and press. Open, fuse a 1" x 21" strip of batting to the wrong side, even with the center fold. Press both edges to the center fold, over the batting. Press strip in half. Edgestitch by machine down both sides of the strip using a matching thread. Repeat for other handle.

Diagram 8

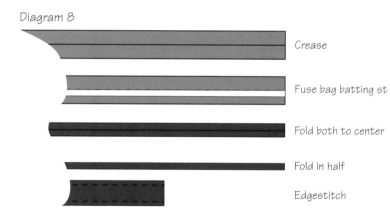

Crease

Fuse bag batting st

Fold both to center

Fold in half

Edgestitch

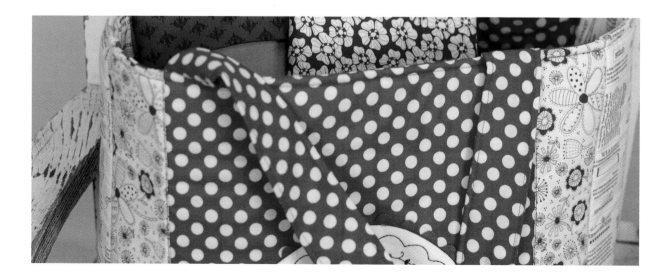

16 Position one handle on the top edge of bag, aligning outer edge of handle with center panel seam (Diagram 9). Baste in place. Repeat with second handle, aligning with handle on front of bag.

17 Turn lining wrong side out. With right sides together, place outer bag inside the lining. Align the top raw edges, match and pin all of the seams along the top edge. Stitch around top edge using a 1/4" seam allowance.

Diagram 9

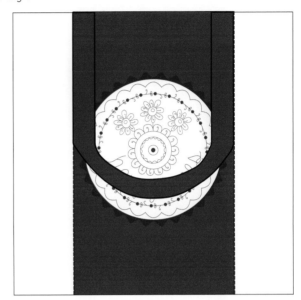

18 Turn the bag right side out by pulling through the opening in the lining. Push out corners and press well. Slip stitch the opening in the lining closed, then push the lining down into the bag smoothly.

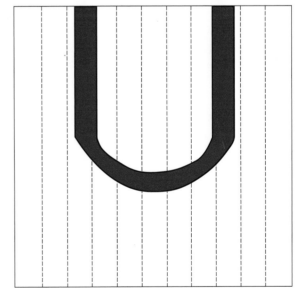

simply social stitching pouch

Bag measures approximately 7-1/2"w x 4"d x 6" h/18 x 10 x 15cm

requirements

1/3 yard/30cm tan fabric

1/3 yard/30cm red fabric

5"/10cm charm squares of 8-10 red fabrics

1" x 14"/35cm lace zipper

Fusible lightweight woven stabilizer

Single sided fusible batting

Sewline Glue Pen, or Roxanne's Glue Baste-It

Pre-cut iron-on 1/2" hexies x 75 (1 pack)

Cottage Garden Perle size 12 #1007 Hugs 'n Kisses red, or other red size 12 Perle cotton.

cutting

From tan fabric cut:

    (1) 9-1/2" x 13" rectangle for bag front

    (1) 6-1/2" x 8-1/2" rectangle for bag back

    (1) 5" x 9" rectangle for bag bottom

From red fabric cut:

    (1) 8-1/2" x 14-1/2" rectangle for lining

    (1) 4-1/2" x 8-1/2" rectangle for pocket

    (1) 3-1/2" x 13" rectangle for zipper panel

    (1) 4" x 6"rectangle for tab

From bag batting cut:

    (1) 5" x 13" rectangle

    (1) 4-3/4"x 13" rectangle

    (1) 1-3/4" x 13" strip

step by step

1 Fold the 9-1/2" x 13" tan fabric in half lengthwise and finger press to form a crease. Transfer design onto fabric using your preferred method (page 9), align the top of the design approximately 1" below fold (Diagram 1).

Diagram 1

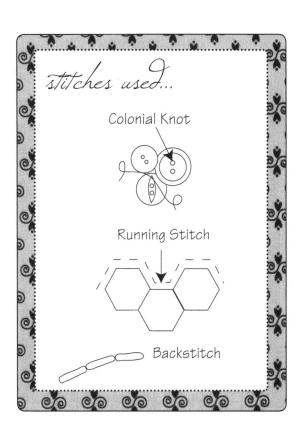

notes...

This is likely the most challenging project in the book. For my English paper pieced hexagons, I used EPP iron-on pre-cut hexagons to make the top of the bag and the bottom band. You can substitute with standard hexagon papers or use a piece of your favorite fabric instead to make the top lid. But pieced hexies are fun and addictive so you may want to try them! The lace zipper simply attaches to the outside of the bag which eliminates any fear of putting in a zipper. It is achievable by all.

2 Fuse a 4-3/4" x 13" piece of stabilizer to the reverse side of the transferred design, aligning it with the fold and the bottom raw edge.

3 Place into an embroidery hoop and stitch over all drawn lines following the embroidery stitch guide (page 11).

4 Prepare and make English paper pieced hexagons following the instructions on page 74. You will need 1 long set of 25 for bottom band and one set of 53 for bag top, following layout in Diagram 2 and Diagram 7 on page 58.

stitches used...

Colonial Knot

Running Stitch

Backstitch

Diagram 2

simply social stitching pouch

front zipper panel

1 Positon the long strip of hexagons along the bottom edge of the stitched panel (Diagram 3). Use small dots of glue to baste in position, or pin baste. Appliqué into place using a matching thread, following instructions on page 73.

2 Stitch a running stitch 1/8" along top edge of the hexie strip. Trim side and bottom edges of hexies back to the edges of the tan fabric (Diagram 4).

3 Fold the bag front in half, wrong sides together, so it measures 4-3/4" x 13".

4 Fold the 3-1/2" x 13" red strip in half, wrong sides together. Open and fuse a 1-3/4" x 13" piece of batting to the wrong side, aligning the batting with one raw edge and opposite along the fold.

5 Butt the edges of the red strip and bag front together, with folded edges touching; pin in place (Diagram 5).

6 Center the lace zipper, face up, on top of folded and pinned edges. Line up zipper teeth on the join. Pin in place (Diagram 6) Using a zipper foot and matching thread, stitch along both sides of the zipper teeth. Check the back to ensure you have stitched through the red and tan layers. Move zipper pull to the center and trim zipper at both ends, taking care not to pull off zipper pull. You may want to stitch across both ends for safety. This completes the front zipper panel.

bag top and back

1 Trace and make one Stitching Pouch Template (page 61). Center over hexie panel (Diagram 7). Mark and trim the edges to the template size.

Diagram 3

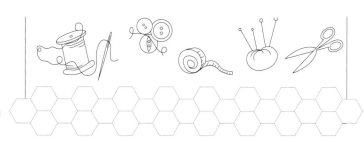

Diagram 4

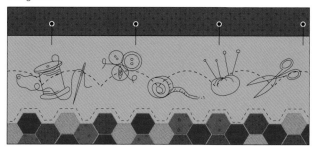

Diagram 5

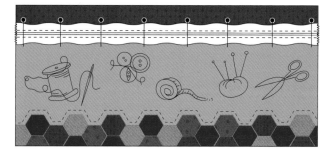

Diagram 6

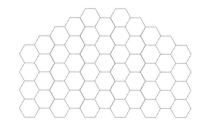

Diagram 7

2 Trim a 5" x 9" tan rectangle to the shape of the curved hexagon panel, using the template from Step 1, or the cut hexie panel.

3 Attach the curved hexagon panel to one side of the 6-1/2" x 8-1/2" tan rectangle. Attach the tan curved panel from step 2 to the opposite side (Diagram 8). Press seams toward rectangle. Fuse a 8-1/2" x 16" rectangle of batting to the wrong side and trim even with unit edges.

bag lining

1 Place outer panel onto the 8-1/2" x 14-1/2" red lining fabric (Diagram 9). Trim even with unit edges. On the lining, mark the two seam lines of the outer bag. Fold at these points and press to make a crease.

2 Double fold one long edge of 4-1/2" x 8-1/2" red rectangle and edgestitch. Position right side down onto lining with raw edge overlapping one of the crease lines 1/4". Stitch on creased line. Press pocket upwards and stitch three vertical lines to make pockets (Diagram 10).

Diagram 8

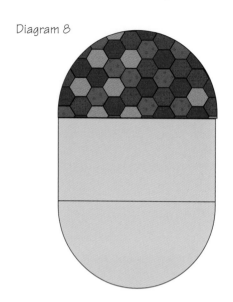

Diagram 9

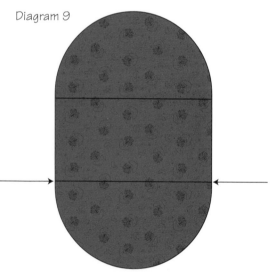

Diagram 10

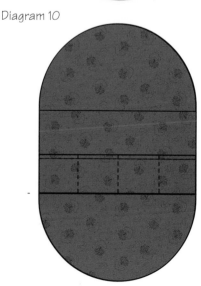

simply social stitching pouch

3 To make the tab, fold and press the 4" x 6" red rectangle in half lengthwise, wrong sides together (Diagram 11). Open and fold both raw edges to meet the center crease, wrong sides together, and press. Fold in half again, matching folded edges. Edgestitch along both sides as shown in Diagram 11.

4 Center the tab, raw edges even with edge of outer bag, right sides together. Baste in place (Diagram 12).

5 With right sides together, center the front zipper panel onto the center section of the outer panel, with zipper and curved hexie panel on same end. The zipper panel will be 1/2" wider than the center of the outer panel. The tab will be sandwiched between the layers (Diagram 13). Stitch side with 1/4" seam allowance. Using very sharp scissors clip carefully into the end points. Repeat this with the other side of the front zipper panel.

6 Carefully ease and pin the bottom curved edge around the long side of the front zipper panel and stitch (Diagram 14).] Open zipper and repeat for the top panel. Stitch and clip curves on top and bottom seams.

Diagram 11

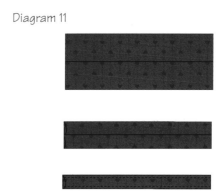

Diagram 12

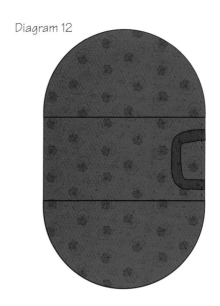

Diagram 13

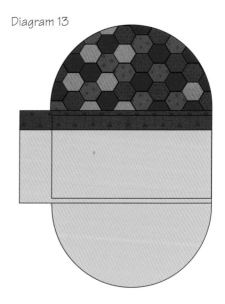

Diagram 14

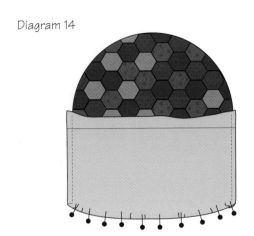

7 Place red lining panel right sides together with the outer panel. Ensure that pocket openings are facing up toward zipper and the hexie panel.

Pin, matching pressed fold lines on the lining to the seam lines of the outer panel. Stitch 1/4" around the outer edge leaving a 5" opening at the bottom edge. Clip curves. Turn right side out by pulling through opening in lining. Slip stitch closed.

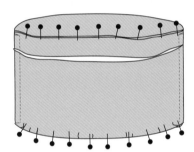

Diagram 15

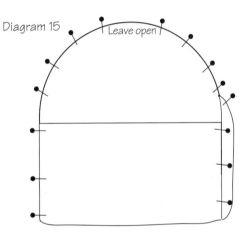

Leave open

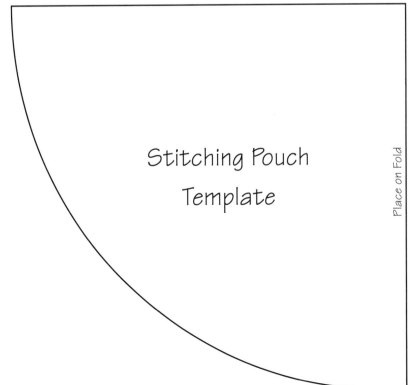

Stitching Pouch
Template

Place on Fold

my mod garden pillow

Cushion measures 13" x 24"/33 x 61cm

requirements

3/4 yard/69cm tan linen

5"/10cm charm squares of six red fabrics

14"/35cm zipper

Fusible lightweight woven stabilizer

Cosmo Perle size 5 thread, or other red
size 5 Perle cotton

cutting

From tan linen cut:
- (1) 11-1/2" x 24-1/2" for pillow front
- (2) 13-1/2" x 13" rectangles for pillow back

From red charms squares cut:
- (12) 2-1/2" squares

step by step

1 Transfer the design onto the 11-1/2" x 24-1/2" piece of linen using your preferred method (page 9).

2 Fuse lightweight woven stabilizer to the back, following manufacturer's instructions. Place into embroidery hoop. Stitch on all drawn lines following the embroidery stitch guide (page 11). Press well.

3 Join the 12 various 2-1/2" red squares together into one row. Attach to the bottom edge of the embroidery panel. Press seams toward the linen.

3 Follow instructions on page 80 for making a zippered cushion back using the two 13-1/2" x 13" rectangles.

4 Insert pillow form or stuff firmly.

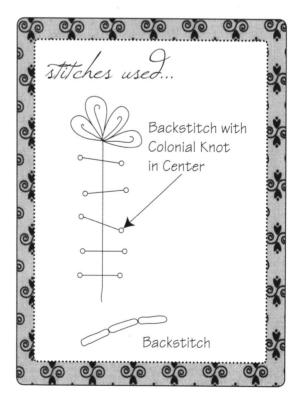

notes...

For this project, I used a different type of thread - Cosmo Perle size 5 in various red shades instead of a single varigated red. This is a much thicker thread so I used a larger needle - a size 5 or 6 crewel needle, so that it would pass through the fabric easily. I used each color randomly and evenly across the design with no particular order or plan. I like how using several subtly different shades of red gives the finished project a little dimension.

stitches used...

Backstitch with Colonial Knot in Center

Backstitch

must have mug bag

Bag measures approximately 6-1/2" x 12-1/2"/16 x 31cm

requirements

5/8 yard/57cm red stripe fabric

1/2 yard/45cm small dot fabric

16—2-1/2"/6.4cm red squares

fusible lightweight batting

Cosmo Seasons #5006, or other variegated red floss

16—1" precut fusible hexagon papers

7/8 yard/80cm red ric rac

cutting

From red stripe fabric cut:
(2) 1-1/2" x 24" strips for pulls
(1) 10-1/2" x 15" rectangle for lining
(1) 4-1/2"x 15" rectangle for top band
(1) 1-1/2" x 15 strip for bottom band

From small dot fabric cut:
(1) 9-1/2" x 15" rectangle for outer bag
(1) 7" x 15" rectangle for inner pocket
(2) circles using Mug Bag Template (page 67)

From fusible batting cut:
(1) 12" x 15" rectangle

preparation

Transfer the design onto the 9-1/2" x 15" small dot fabric using your preferred method (page 9). Use the positioning guides to align.

step by step

1 Lay a 15" piece of ric rac along the bottom edge of the stitchery panel, with edge of ric rac even with edge of fabric. Place the 1-1/2" x 15" red stripe fabric over the top, right sides together, and pin. Sew through all layers securing the ric rac in between. Press toward red stripe fabric.

2 Repeat with another 15" piece of ric rac along the top edge and sew the 4-1/2" x 15"red stripe fabric to the top (Diagram 1). Press toward stitchery panel.

Diagram 1

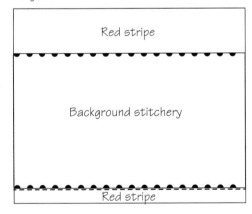

3 Fuse lightweight batting to the wrong side of the pieced unit following manufacturer's instructions.

4 Place the panel into embroidery hoop. Stitch on all drawn lines following the embroidery stitch guide (page 11).

notes...

Many of us have our own special mug we love to use for that perfect cup of tea or coffee. This little mug bag lets you play with redwork and some fun hexies. It will also make you look very clever when you take it to your stitching group, book club gathering or social mums get-together. With inside pockets to hold a tea bag or two, and padding for your special mug, it will impress!

stitches used...

Stem Stitch

Pistol Stitch

Satin Stitch

Backstitch

must have mug bag

5 Following the directions on page 74, stitch together twelve red hexagons into an open ring (Diagram 2). Prepare four extra hexagons for cord tags.

Diagram 2

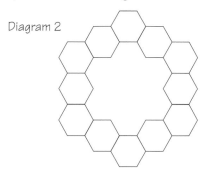

6 Position the hexie ring around the completed embroidery, using Roxanne's Glue-Baste-It, or similar basting glue to hold in place. Stitch into position using matching thread, and a blind appliqué stitch (page 73).

7 For the bag lining, attach the 10-1/2" x 15" red stripe rectangle to the top of the panel (Diagram 3).

Diagram 3

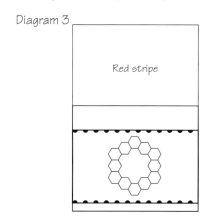

Red stripe

8 For the inner pocket, turn over a double hem 1/2" wide along one long side of the 7" x 15" small dot rectangle. Press and edgestitch using matching thread.

9 Place hemmed piece right side up matching bottom edge of the red stripe bag lining. (Diagram 4). Measure 5" from either side and mark. To make three

pockets, stitch from the top to the bottom at marks, backstitching at both ends to secure. pockets. Baste around the outside edge of pockets.

Diagram 4

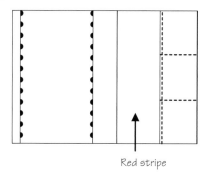

Red stripe

10 Fold in half lengthwise, right sides together, pin, matching seams. Sew together along long edge, leaving a generous opening on the lining side for turning (Diagram 5).

Diagram 5

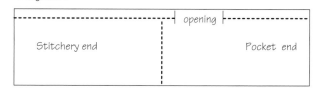

opening

Stitchery end   Pocket end

11 Turn the tube right side out and make a small (1/2") buttonhole just above the top row of ric rac (on the red stripe fabric) on the seam line. Flatten the tube with the seam to one side and mark the opposite fold to make a matching buttonhole.

12 Fuse a small dot circle to a piece of batting and trim to the circular shape. Repeat with second small dot circle. Fold each circle in half and half again and mark the four quarter points on the outside edge. Turn the tube wrong side out and mark the quarter points on both the lining and outer bag ends of the tube. Place a circle right sides together with one end of the tube, pin matching quarter marks on the circle with the quarter marks on bag. Sew around the edge. Repeat on opposite end.

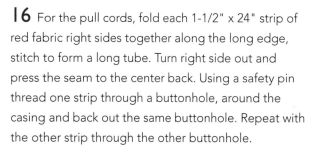

13 Turn the bag right side out by pulling through the opening in the lining; slip stitch closed.

14 Push the lining down into the bag and press. The red fabric at the top of the bag should be folded in half.

15 Stitch in the ditch around the ric rac seam at the bottom of the band. Stitch again approximately 3/4" above this, along the bottom edge of the buttonholes made in step 11 (Diagram 6).

Diagram 6

16 For the pull cords, fold each 1-1/2" x 24" strip of red fabric right sides together along the long edge, stitch to form a long tube. Turn right side out and press the seam to the center back. Using a safety pin thread one strip through a buttonhole, around the casing and back out the same buttonhole. Repeat with the other strip through the other buttonhole.

17 To make cord tab ends – place two prepared hexies right sides together. Whip stitch together around 5 edges of the hexie. Turn through the opening and press. Feed the two ends of a cord into the opening and stitch closed over the cords to secure. Repeat with the other cord on the opposite side.

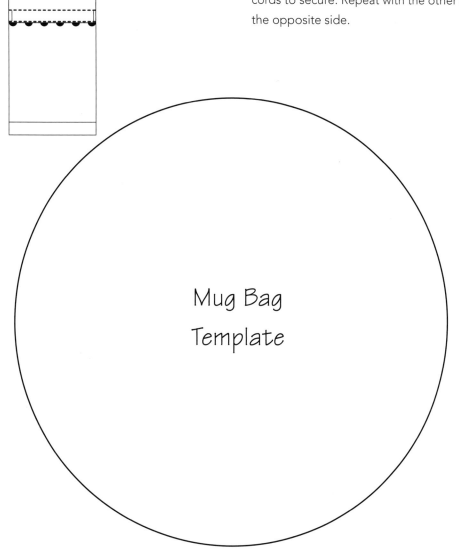

Mug Bag
Template

christmas tag

Decoration measures approximately
4" x 6"/10 x15cm

requirements

7" x 8"/18 x 21cm rectangle red fabric

7" x 8"/18 x 21cm rectangle tan fabric

lightweight woven stabilizer

Cosmo Seasons #5006, or other
variegated red floss

Stiff cardboard

Clear craft glue

10"/25cm twill tape

Hugs 'n Kisses appliqué paper or
other suitable paper

Presencia Finca Perle size 12 cream, or other red
size 12 Perle cotton

Fabric glue pen

preparation

Using templates on page 71, trace and cut two
Large Heart Templates from cardboard, and
two Small Heart Templates from Hugs 'n Kisses
appliqué paper.

step by step

1 Transfer the designs onto the 7" x 8" tan fabric using your preferred method (page 9). Draw the outer cutting line softly; this won't be stitched.

2 Fuse lightweight woven stabilizer to the wrong side of stitchery design tan fabric following manufacturer's instructions and place in embroidery hoop.

3 Stitch over all drawn lines following the embroidery stitch guide (page 11).

4 Press well and cut out on the outer drawn cutting line.

5 Fuse appliqué paper hearts to wrong side of embroidery hearts. Run a line of glue around edge of paper and fold over fabric seam allowance onto the glue. Take care to get smooth curves. Note: for extra help with this gluestick appliqué method you can visit my blog or YouTube channel.

6 Position large heart cardboard onto red fabric and cut fabric leaving a good 1/2" seam allowance; cut two.

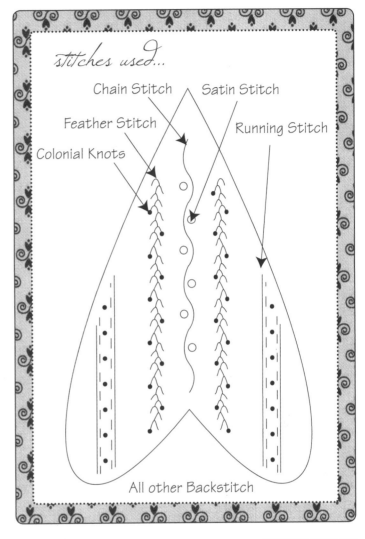

stitches used...

Chain Stitch Satin Stitch

Feather Stitch Running Stitch

Colonial Knots

All other Backstitch

christmas tag

7 Position the embroidered hearts centrally onto a red hearts. Glue baste and appliqué into place using a fine matching thread and appliqué needle. (Appliqué instructions on page 73.)

8 Place a cardboard large heart on wrong side of one red heart. Using clear craft glue fold edges over to the back side and glue tightly. Use pegs or wonderclips to hold until dry.

9 Fold twill tape in half and place into position at the top center of the heart.

10. Place two red hearts wrong sides together. Secure with clear craft glue or hold with wonderclips. Using a #7 crewel needle and the perle thread, join the two sides using a glove stitch. Secure the twill tab as you stitch through it.

Glove Stitch

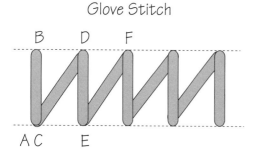

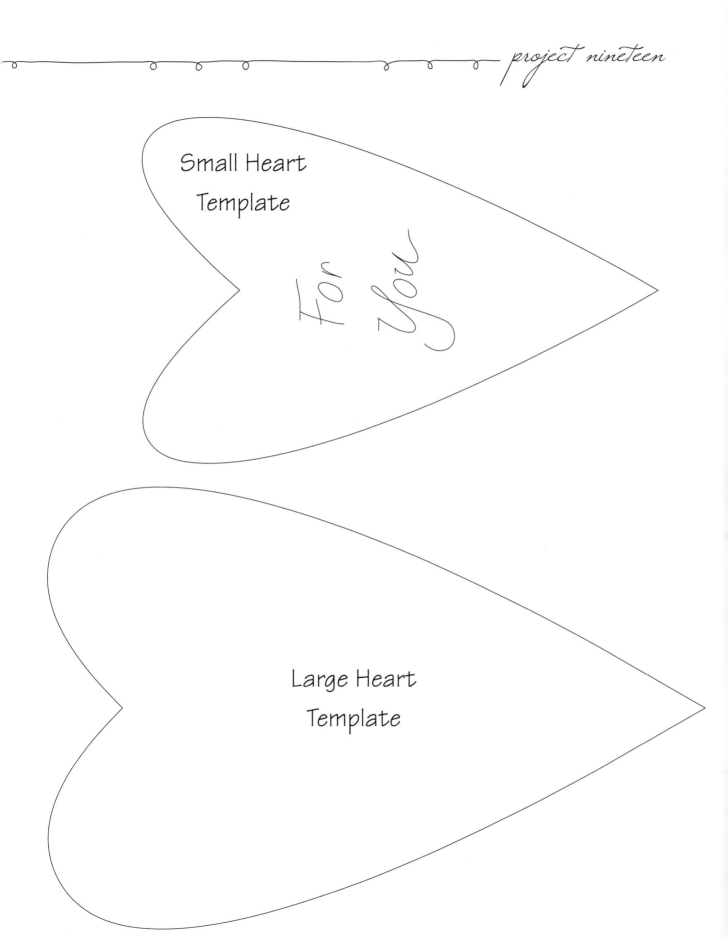

Small Heart
Template

For You

Large Heart
Template

simply redwork basics

general instructions

- Read through all instructions before beginning a project.

- All seams throughout the book are 1/4" unless otherwise stated. Seam allowances are included in the measurements given in the cutting instructions.

- Fabric requirements are based on 100% cotton fabric, non-directional, 40"/100cm useable width.

- Fabric notes have been included to aid in fabric selection.

- Backing fabric and batting may not always be included in the requirements for cushions. Refer to cushion options, page 79, to calculate requirements.

- The projects are easily cut and most accurately made using a rotary cutter, ruler and cutting mat.

- Fabrics are placed right sides together unless otherwise stated in the instructions.

appliqué

Some projects in this book require a motif or shape to be appliquéd to a background. To do this by hand, I use a Hugs 'n Kisses appliqué needle and a strong, fine thread (my preference is Superior Bottom Line - a 60 wt poly thread). Use a color that matches or blends with the fabric of your appliqué piece and stitch with a blind appliqué stitch.

Blind or Applique Stitch

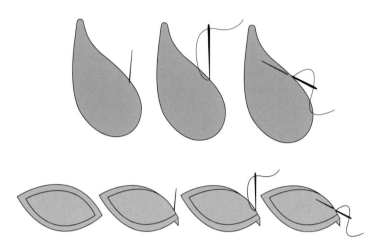

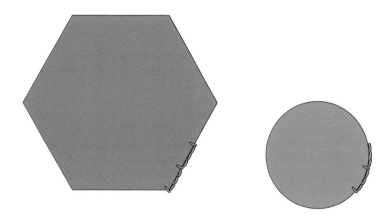

To appliqué by machine I use a monofilament thread (I prefer Superior Monopoly), an open toe embroidery foot and a blind hem stitch.

For more assistance on appliqué the Hugs 'n Kisses way view my YouTube videos on this method or see my Simply Appliqué book for more detailed instructions.

simply redwork basics

english paper piecing

My English paper piecing (EPP) method uses precut iron-on paper shapes which can be left in the project and washed to dissolve. You choose to use your own hexagon paper piecing method.

- Fuse precut hexie paper to wrong side of fabric with a hot iron, leaving 1/2" seam allowance between papers.

- Cut out with scissors leaving a 1/4" seam allowance around each edge.

- Run a line of fabric glue (I use a Sewline™ glue pen) along one edge of the paper template. Fold the seam allowance inwards until you feel the edge of the paper and then press down onto the glue. Repeat for each side. Prepare all required hexagons.

- Join shapes by placing right sides together and whip stitching using a strong, fine thread and a Hugs 'n Kisses appliqué needle or a needle of your choice.

- Once motif is complete, position onto background fabric, glue baste into place and appliqué into position, using an appliqué needle and strong, fine thread.

- If using as a complete paper pieced panel, position template over top of pieced motif, trim around template shape and sew into your project as if it were fabric.

Hexies

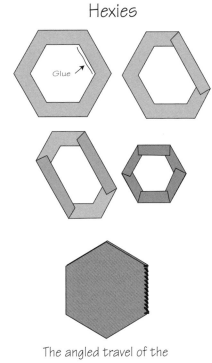

The angled travel of the thread is on the wrong side

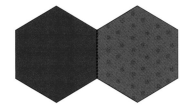

From the front you should barely see the stitches

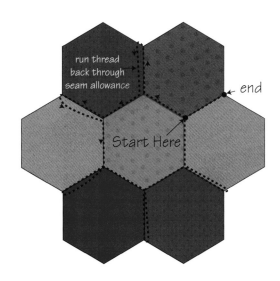

run thread back through seam allowance

end

Start Here

74

layering a quilt

Cut backing fabric and batting at least 4-8" larger than your quilt top.

- Lay the freshly pressed backing wrong side up on floor or work surface, smooth out any wrinkles so that it is perfectly flat. Use masking or painter's tape to tape the edges to the floor or table. It should be flat and taut. Do not stretch it.

- Lay the batting on top of the backing, smooth out with sweeping hands, being careful not to move or pull the backing fabric. If you're using a packaged batting that's been folded, let it rest out of the pack to remove any creases prior to using.

- Center the well pressed quilt top, right side up, on the batting and backing. Be sure that both the backing and batting are several inches larger than the quilt top on all sides.

- Beginning at the center, baste the three layers together, either with a needle and strong thread or with good quality safety pins. Pin or hand baste the entire quilt in a grid pattern approximately 4" apart. If pinning, you may leave the pins open until the entire top is pinned, then close them, or you may close as you go. Try to avoid pinning where you intend to quilt. It will make things a little easier in the quilting process.

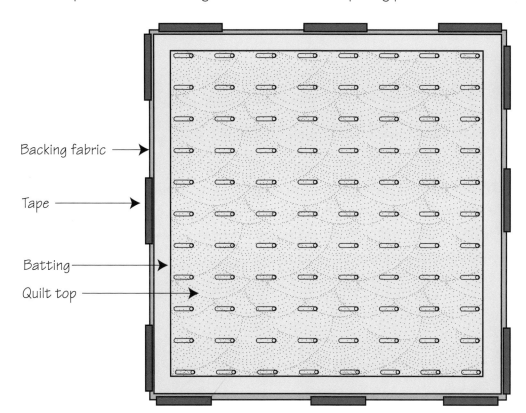

Backing fabric

Tape

Batting

Quilt top

simply redwork basics

quilting

I could write a whole book on quilting, and there are many places you can get information. This will be a simple explanation of quilting.

There are two main types of quilting:

- **Straight line:** normally, straight line quilting is done with a walking foot. The feed dogs of your sewing machine push the quilt sandwich through the machine and the selected stitch setting determines your even stitch length.

- **Free motion quilting:** done with a free motion or darning foot with the feed dogs lowered so that the quilt sandwich is free to move in any direction. The speed you move the quilt, along with the speed of your machine, determines the stitch length.

You can use a vast array of threads. On the projects in this book, I used a matching thread that blends with the fabric. You may choose to use a contrasting or specialty thread if you desire. You can also use an invisible monofilament thread for projects where you do not want your quilting featured. You may need to test your tension with different threads until you are satisfied with the resulting stitch.

As a general rule, always stitch the longest stabilizing rows first. This may be in the ditch of horizontal and vertical seams, or 1/4" from seams in straight rows.

I free-motion quilt along the outer edge of appliquéd pieces using either invisible thread or a thread that matches the background fabric. You can then simply quilt a filler design in the background to make the appliqué pop. The amount of quilting required can also be determined by the type of batting you have chosen to use. Some batting requires much denser quilting than others. Check the manufacturer's recommended spacing.

If you decide to have your tops quilted by a longarm quilter remember to provide backing and batting at least 4" larger on all sides. Always check for this and any other special requirements from your quilter.

binding and mitered joins

Diagram 1

I cut binding strips 2-1/2" wide on the straight grain of the fabric for a finished 1/2" double bind. I prefer to miter the strips to make one long strip. Mitered joins are a good way to lessen bulk in the binding.

Fold all binding strips in half and lay them on a straight line on a cutting mat. Cross the ends over the 45-degree line. Lay ruler along line and cut. Place two strip ends right sides together and stitch with a 1/4" seam, taking care not to stretch the bias seam. (Diagram 1).

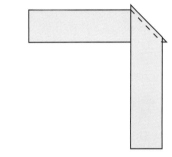

hanging sleeve

Whether a wallhanging or a quilt, it is always easier to attach a hanging sleeve before you bind it.

Cut a strip of fabric approximately 6-9" wide and the same width as your finished quilt. Turn in a double hem at both short ends and stitch. Press the strip in half wrong sides together. Align on the back of the quilt, raw edges along the top of the quilt. Baste. When attaching the binding to the front, you will secure the sleeve in the stitch line. After handstitching the binding to the back of your quilt you can handstitch the bottom edge of the sleeve with a stitch going through the backing fabric only.

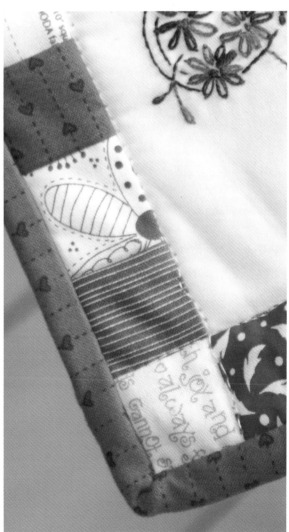

simply redwork basics

attaching mitered binding corners & joins

Press the binding strips in half, wrong sides together. Starting mid way on one side of quilt sandwich, pin binding strip on quilt top, aligning binding edges with the edges of quilt top. Leave a 10" tail. Sew, using a 1/4" seam allowance. (A walking foot is sometimes beneficial to use when attaching binding). Stop sewing 1/4" from first corner and backtack. Remove quilt from under presser foot.

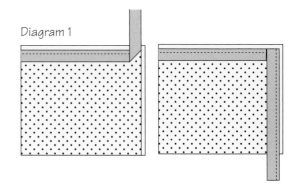

Diagram 1

Fold the binding strip up and then back down on itself to square the corner (Diagram 1). Place the quilt back under the presser foot and continue sewing from the edge of the quilt to the next corner. Repeat this process until you reach approximately 12" from your starting point.

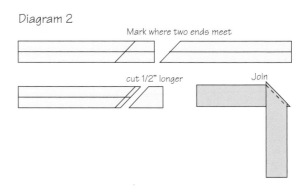

Diagram 2

Mark where two ends meet

cut 1/2" longer   Join

Bring the two ends of your binding together. Open out flat and position the strips on top of each other. Mark the edge of your starting strip. Trim the other end 1/2" longer than your mark (Diagram 2).

Place the two bias cuts right sides together and stitch 1/4" seam. Finger press the seam open, fold the binding in half again. Reposition under your presser foot and stitch the remaining piece of binding.

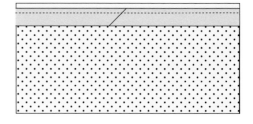

Trim corners and the edge of the batting and backing to 1/2" from the stitching line. Turn the binding to the back of the quilt, pin and slipstitch covering the stitching line, using a matching thread. As you get to each corner, fold the miters evenly and stitch the diagonal seams.

cushion options

I have used various methods when making the cushion projects in this book. Follow my instructions here or choose your preferred method to complete your cushions.

envelope method

Cut two rectangles of backing fabric referring to the the cutting instructions given for the cushion front. Cut the rectangles approximately two thirds the size so they will overlap. For example, If the front is 16" x 16", cut two pieces 10" x 16".

Double hem along one long side of each piece. Turn under a 1/2" and press, turn under another 1/2" and press again. With matching thread, edgestitch 1/8" from folded edge and again 3/8" from folded edge.

Note: You may wish to overlock (serge) or zig zag all other raw edges of your cushion top and backing.

Place cushion front right side up on a flat surface. Place one backing piece on top right side down and raw edges even (Diagram 1). Place the remaining piece in the same manner at the opposite side of the pillow front (Diagram 2). The two pieces will overlap by approximately one third.

Pin all edges. Stitch around all four sides. Trim corners at an angle, turn through the opening, push out corners and press well. Insert a pillow form.

envelope with backing and binding

Cut and hem cushion backing pieces as you would for the previous method. Position the two backing pieces overlapped as before but WRONG sides together with the cushion front. Pin or baste outside edges 1/8" from edge of fabric.

Make binding long enough for all four sides of your cushion plus 4". Attach binding to front of cushion sandwich following the directions for binding on page 77-78. Turn to back and slip stitch into place.

Diagram 1

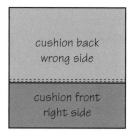

cushion back
wrong side

cushion front
right side

Diagram 2

Baste or pin

Diagram 3

Stitch and trim corners

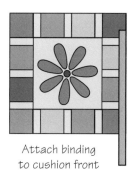

Attach binding
to cushion front

zippered back

Cut a backing piece of fabric the same size as the front plus 1". Cut in half.

Using a zipper 2" longer than the width of the cushion, place the zipper, pull side down, on the right side of one back piece; with the edge of the zipper even with the raw edge of the fabric. Using a zipper foot, stitch as close as possible to the zipper teeth. Press open and edge stitch. Repeat on the other side of the zipper with the second piece of backing.

Open zipper pull to about half way. Place cushion back and front right sides together. Stitch around all sides, trimming corners at an angle. Trim excess zipper ends and turn right side out by pulling through zipper opening. Push out corners, press well and insert cushion form.

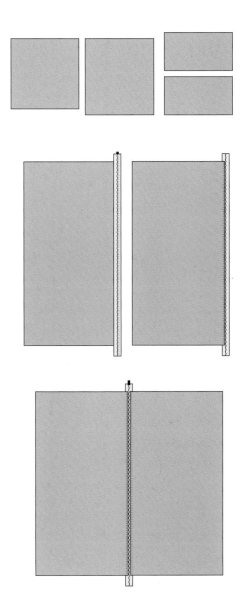